The more nervous speakers are initially, the more potential they have to become amazing.

"I doubt there is anyone out there who has not, at some point, been scared to death about public speaking. In fact, for most of us, it is always a daunting and frightening prospect. That's why *Flip the Fear of Public Speaking* by Julianne Kissack is a book worth reading – worth inhaling, digesting and referring to over and over again. The author, a successful registered nurse, overcame her own deep and extreme speaking phobia and, thankfully, has documented and passed her battle plan on to the rest of us. *Flip the Fear of Public Speaking* – read it and leave the heart palpitations for other occasions."

Simon T. Bailey
Author of *Release Your Brilliance* and *The Vuja de Moment*

"Julianne Kissack's *Flip The Fear of Public Speaking* not only shows you how to overcome your nerves but also how to structure and deliver speeches that will energize, entertain, and inspire all of your future audiences. Don't go into your next speech without it."

Craig Valentine
1999 World Champion of Public Speaking
Author of *World Class Speaking*

"I know Julianne as a prominent member of the Oxford Speakers Club. Julianne is a truly excellent speaker and has the impressive capability of engaging an audience through truly expressive speaking. As well as having mastered all the basic component skills of brilliant speaking Julianne exhibits thought leadership in this field. In particular, her novel principles of, 'Dare to disturb the universe' and 'Speak in the moment' are quite unique. Julianne is keen to share these principles with others." *May 15, 2010*

Paul Ovington
MBA, MSc, PRINCE2, MSP, DipM, DTM,
Area Governor Area 7 (Oxfordshire), Toastmasters International

"I highly recommend Julianne Kissack and *Flip the Fear of Public Speaking* to anyone looking to turn their fear of speaking into a definite advantage in positively influencing and winning over an audience."

Richard Burton
SMART Technologies

"EASE - the word that best describes Julianne. Easy to Listen to - with true-life experiences and anecdotes passing into the lessons learned. Easily Understood - the messages, tips, techniques are readily accepted by her audience. Easy to Implement - practical and immediate solutions that will improve the lives of her audience for the better."

Palmo Carpino
Creator of *from Pen to Platform*

Flip the Fear

of Public

Speaking:

Five Proven Principles

Julianne Kissack RNBN, MBA

Published by Kissack & Kissack

Kissack & Kissack Inc.
300, 85 Shawville Blvd. SE
P.O. Box 18018 Shawnessy PO
Calgary, AB T2Y 3W0

First Edition 2012

ISBN 978-0-9881384-0-7

To Lloyd and Gloria Kissack, who first, and have always, inspired me to Flip my Fear

TABLE OF CONTENTS

INTRODUCTION

Courage is resistance to fear, mastery of fear—not absence of fear.

– Mark Twain (1835 – 1910)

I am terrified.

As I walk slowly into the room the fear grows worse. Adrenaline hits my bloodstream and the room begins to tilt. "Boom, boom, boom." My heart threatens to beat through my chest. Someone speaks behind me. "What?" I say. I cannot concentrate over the noise of my heart and the speed at which things seem to be moving. Again, the voice, "Julianne you will be fourth, all right?"

"Um, sure." My voice is weak and strained. It feels as if I have a hundred cotton balls in my mouth. My tongue is dry and sticky, hands cold and sweaty. I take them off the desk now supporting me and wipe them down the front of my jeans. A big sweaty print of my hand remains on the desk.

The desk again becomes my support as I sit down, a prisoner as the cell door slams shut. A dark black pencil mark grabs my attention. I try wiping it away with my shirtsleeve, ignoring the sound of excited voices entering the room. I look up at the clock and see the "tick, tick, tick" of the second hand, speeding up the moments before the class begins. *Is this what it feels like to die?* My stomach sinks. Thoughts start to race. *What if my face turns so red that people laugh? What if I actually faint and hit my head? What will everyone think when they hear my voice shake?* The skin on my face burns beneath the extra three coats of concealing makeup I applied this morning. Panic rises up again and I taste acrid bile from my stomach burning the back of my throat. I inhale deeply, spreading the feeling of panic throughout my chest. My eyes grow wide searching for the door. It is still open. I could run now.

Mrs. Hill walks over at that moment, and I watch my hallway freedom disappear into smaller slivers. Then, "click" and the door shuts. My heart beats a faster, shallower rhythm: "Bump, bump, bump, bump."

"Okay class," Mrs. Hill begins, "As you know, today we are finishing up the last of our presentations to conclude the section on Shakespeare. First we will have Jenna, then Patrick, Steven, and finally Julianne…"

Just like it was yesterday, I remember sitting in Mrs. Hill's classroom, her hands folded on her desk as she watched students walking up to the front of the room one by one to deliver their grade-eleven English 20 presentations. I visualize the clock on the wall above the door and the navy-and-white-striped tank top I was wearing, carefully selected to draw the least amount of attention to my face, knowing for sure it would turn bright red. It is still clear because of the sheer strength of my terror at the thought of delivering the presentation. It was a defining moment in my life. I knew that if I wanted to be successful in any career after high school it would mean encountering and living through similar situations.

It amazes me now that the thought of presenting in that classroom evoked such a strong reaction. But it led me through a process of overcoming the fear of public speaking and finally to write this book because I learned that it can be overcome. The fear of public speaking can be "flipped" and turned into enthusiasm, energy, and the power to persuade an audience. It can be used by speakers not only in successful speaking, but also to reach whatever goals they put forward in their lives. Flipping the fear is a transferable skill that can be used repeatedly to challenge barriers that block success. Whether used in a person's personal or professional life, it presents a valuable and powerful tool.

For those just starting the process of "flipping the fear" of public speaking, this book is a summary of five of the most effective principles I have learned through years of challenging my own fear and flipping terror into positive energy and enthusiasm.

Very sincerely,

Julianne Kissack

CHAPTER 1

"Speaking In the Moment"

Go confidently in the direction of your dreams. Live the life you've imagined.

– Henry David Thoreau

Please read the following two examples and concentrate on your reaction while reading them.

Example number one:

It was the first day of grade-six and I awoke feeling excited that it had finally arrived. Dressed in the new school clothes that my mom and I had bought the week before and that had been hanging neatly in my closet ever since, I rushed through breakfast and ran out the door and most of the way to school. I was eager to see my friends and hear about their summer adventures.

It was halfway through the morning session when Mr. Payton, our gym teacher, walked through the door and told us that it was the grade-six foot race that day and that we would all be racing in the schoolyard during lunch. I had waited for years for a chance to run in the race, every year watching the grade-six girls line up and race across the field. Now it was my turn. As the time came closer, I grew more and more nervous. We marched outside and Mr. Payton had all of us line up at the start of the race and get in our set positions before he blew the whistle to start us off.

After running as fast as I had ever tried, to my amazement Mr. Payton yelled to me across the field that I had won the race. I was on top of the world and liked the feeling.

Example number two:

My eyes fly open and my heart is already pounding adrenaline through my veins. Today is the day—the first day of grade-six. Instantly awake, I throw back the covers. *Finally.* I gingerly take the new purple shirt and dark blue jeans, stored perfectly in the closet off of their hangers and proudly pull them on. I feel the new fabric against my skin and deeply inhale their newness as I stand up straight. *I am ready.*

As I walk down the old familiar street to school, everything bustles with excitement. I see children leaving their houses all along the street and hear excited cries when they meet friends. The air feels cool and crisp on my face, expanding my lungs as I draw in a breath. The sun shines brightly through the trees, some still green and alive and many more turning bright yellow and orange. I hear leaves crunching under my feet, and the smell of sap hits me, reminding me it is fall.

It is still early when I reach the school and keenly take my place at a new desk. My stomach dances and I can't get the grin off of my face when I look around and see my friends filing into the room. Halfway through the morning session the classroom door opens. Mr. Payton, the gym teacher, makes an announcement. "Girls, get ready. After this class you will be running the grade-six foot race." He looks around the room, smiles, and then shuts the door. *Of course!* I had forgotten. *The grade-six foot race is today.* My heart starts beating faster as I take a sharp breath. *It is finally my turn. I have been waiting for years, and it is finally my turn.* I walk outside to the gym field with the other girls, and I feel my new jeans getting hot and starting to stick to my legs. *Why did I wear jeans today?* I try to stretch them out as I walk. Instead, the fabric just starts to feel heavier, and I feel a drop of sweat drip down my leg.

"Okay girls, line up!" yells Mr. Payton. Time starts to stand still. I hear the girls on either side of me as we approach the faded white chalk starting line. It sits between grass patches on the field. I can hear the air entering and leaving the other girls' lungs. Their breathing grows faster. *Gulp.* We line up. I look down at the dirt and see a tiny blade of grass poking through the broken white line. My hands feel the dryness of the ground as I take my position. "Get ready!" yells Mr. Payton. I focus and my breath almost stops. All I can hear is the slow and firm beat of my heart in my ears. Every muscle in my body is tense and waiting. Time feels like forever. "Bang" goes the start gun. My arms come up, powerfully moving me forward off the line. My feet dig into the dirt and my legs spring into action. My head is focused straight ahead and my eyes are set on the goalpost sixty yards down the field. My breath is fast and forced out in rhythm with my footsteps, "ph ph ph." My feet touch the ground and fly off again. I feel strong and light like I am flying. Then I am past the goalpost and my feet and arms are slowing. My breath is heavier and burns down to the bottom of my lungs. A new feeling of relief comes over me as I look up at the sky. *I did it.*

I ran it.

"Nice work, girl." I hear from across the field. "You won," yells Mr. Payton. I can feel my face relax for a moment and then realize what he said. I can't help but smile. Success hits my body. I like it.

These two examples are different. The second example is longer and told in present rather than past tense. But more than that, the intent is to allow readers to feel more emotion in the second example and to bring the reader into the moments experienced through telling the story. If you felt the runner's emotion in the second example and had a sense of experiencing the anxiety and exhilaration of running the grade-six foot race, then you have successfully experienced the first principle of flipping the fear: "Speaking in the Moment."

The purpose of "Speaking in the Moment" is not only to bring an audience into the speaker's experience, but it also helps the speaker flip the fear by channeling nervous energy into positive energy and enthusiasm.

"Speaking in the Moment" takes a speaker into their own experience and allows them to focus on relating to the audience, rather than concentrating on what they are trying to say or how they are trying to speak. For many speakers, the most anxiety-producing experience results when a) they are not overly familiar with the information they are presenting and b) when they are trying to read unfamiliar material from a script or visual presentation. Both instances make speakers pay more attention to what might happen if they lose their place, forget words, or lose control of their voice. Any of the three can make them lose connection with the audience. Conversely, when speaking in the moment, speakers are not worrying about forgetting content because they are already experts. This frees the speaker to relive the experience with the audience and to concentrate on relating the moment and creating strong connections with the audience. It is in this moment that a speaker's energy is directed outward through enthusiasm rather than inward, which adds only nervous energy. The outward, enthusiastic projection results in liberation from fear, making it an enjoyable speaking experience.

I first experienced "flipping the fear" of public speaking at a Dale Carnegie course where I was encouraged to "be in the moment" and relate an experience to the audience. I stood up in front of the forty people in the room with my knees shaking and face red. In my mind I went back to my first day of grade-six and started to feel the emotions I had walking to school. When I reached the part of running the grade-six foot race, I could feel my voice grow stronger and had my courage to actually look the audience in the eye. I was amazed and enjoying it. For the first time in my life of public speaking I wasn't focused on worrying about my face turning red or whether I would remember the next part of my speech. I was back in time reliving the feelings of success experienced when I won that grade-six foot race so many years ago.

After learning this principle, it is important to relive a chosen experience in as much detail as possible and to begin channeling any nervous energy toward connecting with the audience. Since the speaker is already an expert in the speech's content, an added benefit of this principle means less time preparing or writing a speech. Time, a major barrier for challenging the fear of public speaking, can be maximized. The strength of "Speaking in the Moment" allows a speaker to become a topic expert with little preparation. I have found "Speaking in the Moment" so effective and useful that it allows me to prepare a speech in about five minutes and to deliver it in a way that people think I have been practicing for weeks.

Choosing a moment that had a profound impact means that the speaker will more clearly be able to remember the moment and, therefore, more easily relive it with an audience.

Public speaking can be intimidating, and to some speaking in the moment might sound terrifying. How does a new speaker stand up in front of a group and start speaking in the moment without experience?

Although the details were never taught in any course I took, the first step is to pick a moment to share. For best results, pick a time with a deep and lasting impression. Think of memories that have remained because they made you feel extremely happy, sad, angry, or jubilant. Then, think of the event leading up to the experienced emotion. Once the moment is clear, the rest is easy. Sometimes to prepare for a "Speaking in the Moment" speech, I will sit down with pen and paper and write out the experience, and I encourage you to do the same. Start by asking the following questions to help bring that moment to life. It is important to concentrate on the felt emotion in that moment:

- Do I feel elated?
- Do I feel content?
- Do I feel satisfied?
- Am I glowing?
- Do I feel confident?
- Am I laughing?
- Am I crying?
- Am I angry or upset?

Once connected with the emotion, describe in detail what happened on paper similar to the way it will be presented. Make certain to use your own perspective, and from that place write as if you are speaking to the audience. The key to this is to concentrate on using the five senses within the description. This means starting sentences using words such as "I feel," "I see," "I hear," "I touch," "I smell," and "I think" rather than "I remember when I felt…" or "I saw a man on the street." Take the audience into the moment by relating to them right then: "I feel terrified!" or "I see a man in front of me. He is tall and dark and has a crooked smile on his lips." Immediately, the audience is with you in the moment because they can see and feel your experience.

Start this process by answering the following questions, and frame the writing using the sentence starters "I see," "I feel," "I hear," "I smell," "I taste," and "I think."

- Where am I?
- Who is around me?
- What am I doing? What are they doing?
- How am I feeling? Is this feeling growing?
- What do I see besides the people with me?
- What kinds of colors, textures, buildings, and objects are around me?
- What can I hear? What is being said? What is the background sound?
- What can I smell?
- What can I taste?
- What can I touch?
- Do I have anything in my hands? Am I holding something?
- Are my arms and legs in motion and how does this feel?
- Am I smiling or what other expression do I have on my face?

Once started in this process, the moment should begin to come alive on the page as it did in the second story I told at the beginning of this chapter.

Note: Starting consecutive sentences with "I" can weaken a speech. Use the exercise to frame the speech in the first person. Then, when polishing the speech, drop excessive use of "I" while remaining in the present tense.

The next step is deciding who the audience will be. Initially this might be a wall in the bedroom, the mirror in a bathroom, or a family member once he or she has come home from work or school. Or, it might be the local Toastmasters group with the challenge to sign up for that ever-intimidating Icebreaker speech.

It's a good sign when speakers feel intimidated. The more nervous speakers are initially, the more potential they have to become amazing. Although "Speaking in the Moment" is really a fairly advanced speaking skill and takes time to practice effectively, it is also what I have found to be the most useful tool in "flipping the fear" of public speaking. Although it might sound confusing at first, try to think about the technique in a simple way. Keep in mind that initial success doesn't require starting with a large or intimidating audience. Start speaking to the bedroom wall before progressing to the bathroom mirror and eventually to another living, breathing human—with potentially a dog or cat in between. When the time is right, you will be ready to challenge yourself to speak in front of groups.

Speaking in the Moment Exercise:

1. Summarize the speech topic in one sentence. An easy way to get started is to think about a simple question, such as: "What I would do if I won the lottery." This can later be used as the speech title:

   _____

   _____

   _____

2. With the topic in mind, place yourself "in the moment" and describe three points for each of the senses below with as much detail as possible:

   I see:

   1. _____

   2. _____

   3. _____

   I hear:

   1. _____

   2. _____

   3. _____

   I feel:

   1. _____

   2. _____

   3. _____

I smell:

1. _____

2. _____

3. _____

I taste:

1. _____

2. _____

3. _____

I think:

1. _____

2. _____

3. _____

In the next chapter, methods of productively channeling speaking anxiety will be explored...

CHAPTER 2

"Dare to Disturb the Universe"

"And indeed there will be time

To wonder, "Do I dare?" and, "Do I dare?"

Time to turn back and descend the stair,

With a bald spot in the middle of my hair. . .

Do I dare

Disturb the universe?"

– T.S. Eliot

Surviving the process of contemplating delivering a presentation and learning to "Speak in the Moment" in the previous chapter is intimidating. At this point it is important to put fear into perspective. This can be done using the second principle: "Dare to Disturb the Universe."

After reading this paragraph, close your eyes and picture the expanse of the universe over time. Imagine space stretching out infinitely through time and ruler marks showing different points of time in history, such as when dinosaurs roamed the earth, when humans still lived in caves, and when the first car was invented. This all stretches across millions and millions of years. Along the ruler marks, picture what stands out as defining historical moments. A speaker might picture some of the things just mentioned, or perhaps an ice age, either recent World Wars, or the innovation of the Internet. In order to make an impact or a mark in history, the event had to be pretty significant. Take the image forward in time along that ruler past the present and millions of years into the future. If someone else is looking back at history, what do they see?

This visual is helpful for two reasons. First, it puts the presentation a speaker has to do next month, tomorrow, or this afternoon into perspective and begs a speaker to ask: "In the grand scheme of things, is the fact that my face might go red or my voice might shake or falter during this presentation so important that it is worth all of this nervous energy? If I am merely a split second in time (according to the timeline ruler) and this presentation even less so, should I really worry about my face or voice, or should I be more focused on the actual impact of my message?" Second, this visual asks the speaker to consider this: "If I really do want to make an impact greater than this moment in time, I am going to have to expand some major energy to even begin to make a mark on that timeline."

I first heard the phrase "Dare to Disturb the Universe" when a classmate read the poem by T.S. Eliot entitled "The Love Song of J. Alfred Prufrock." In the poem, Prufrock poses the question "Do I dare disturb the universe?" I was sitting on the floor of the classroom and can remember how inspired my classmate's face appeared as he read the poem. At the time it brought to mind the image of that ruler and made me think, *Wow, I am so small in this great big place that if I want to be heard or noticed or if I want to do something special in this world, it is going to have to be big.* Keeping that thought alive has allowed me to put speaking into perspective, either before or after a speech. It has allowed me to look back at the moment I sat in Ms. Hill's grade-eleven class, heart pounding and adrenaline rushing, to think, *Hey, that was nothing. What I have accomplished since is so much bigger. How much farther can I go?* When I consider the poem today, it also instills a sense of urgency to not just sit still and ponder taking action or let fear stand in the way, but to do something now.

The real purpose of this principle contains two main parts:

1. When people jump out of their comfort zones by attempting to "disturb the universe" with the impact of a particular message, they automatically increase energy and enthusiasm as they speak. The benefit is that it brings fear felt on the inside to the outside where it can be controlled and used as energy and enthusiasm to connect with the audience. Fear is energy. Some speakers might feel enthusiastic but fail to convey enthusiasm to the audience. That's because approximately only ten percent of the energy people think is coming across to an audience actually gets there. In order to achieve one hundred percent energy that shows, speakers need to put out 1000 percent energy. Talk about attempting to disturb the universe!

(If 100 percent input = 10 percent output, then 100 percent output = 1000 percent input.)

2. "Daring to Disturb the Universe" will automatically bring more power and conviction to a message. It happens by channeling energy constructively. This doesn't mean speakers need to jump around on stage and wave their arms in an attempt to mark a line in history. Energy can be channeled in different ways, specifically through any of the following:

   a. Body language. In certain instances, this can mean jumping around on stage and waving arms. It can also mean slight but purposeful movements.
   b. The tone and volume of voice as well as strategic silent pauses.
   c. The words chosen.

The key to successful use of "Dare to Disturb the Universe" is congruence. This means that an emotion is portrayed through all signals sent to the audience. For example, to illustrate the emotion of anger, speakers are not going to speak in quiet tones with eyes averted to the floor standing in one spot. Instead, they are going to speak loudly, perhaps wave their arms, stomp their feet, raise their voice, and look the audience straight in the eye as they make a point. Conversely, if they want to portray the emotion of joy, they might still use louder tones, but perhaps lighter and with more inflection to illustrate joy and enthusiasm.

They might also use light and open body language, such as opening their arms to express how happy they are feeling or skipping across the floor with their face turned upwards.

These are both extreme examples that might not be appropriate when standing up in a boardroom to deliver a technical presentation or weekly project report, speaking at a friend's wedding, or participating in other more somber speaking events. However, this principle can be used in more formal settings. President Obama delivering a State of the Union address demonstrated an effective example of formal use of "Dare to Disturb the Universe." During the address, The President proclaimed that he "Hated the bailout of Wall Street," and stated it several times. Every time he used the word "hated" he used purposeful body language by punctuating the word with a direct arm movement. His message was very powerful, not because The President was jumping across the stage and waving his arms, but because the movement he used was purposeful. His body language matched the powerful word choice and also his use of silence. The word "hated" is congruent with direct arm movements and matches the firm, strong tone of voice.

What matters is that a speaker is congruent for all emotions and movements during a speech.

It's also helpful to think of becoming larger than the moment to alleviate anxiety and to realize that if a speaker wants to make a difference then being nervous won't do. All nervous energy needs to be channeled into congruently delivering the message to make an impact.

The first step in "Daring to Disturb the Universe" is to put the speech that is causing anxiety into perspective. Does it really matter overall if an audience might notice the speaker is a bit nervous? Even if the worst happened, say a speaker fainted dead on stage and was carted off, what would be the worst result? It would surely cause the speaker a bit of embarrassment. However, in the grand scheme of things would it really be worth the amount of fear and energy required to cause the speaker to faint?

Note that a form of energy is still at work. The symptoms of nervousness that a person thinks are painfully visible to the audience are actually coming across as only about ten percent of what the speaker imagines. In an interesting experiment try this: the next time you deliver a presentation and feel nervous, ask someone in the audience afterwards what they noticed. It is guaranteed they will have not noticed half of the symptoms you felt and definitely not as severely as you imagined.

I learned this concept through a painful experience. A year into my career as a healthcare consultant I was asked to facilitate a working group session. The purpose of the session was to gather clinicians, who were experts in a particular service, and to gain their opinion on five specific areas of proposed service change. A month prior I had facilitated a successful working group with the same clinicians. Also, having regularly spoken with two Toastmasters groups and recently facilitated a Dale Carnegie course as a Group Leader, I was feeling very confident in my ability to speak in front of an audience. Right up until the session started I was confident that it would be as successful as the last. Then something strange happened. When the session started and I stood up to introduce myself and recap the previous session, my face and neck began feeling hot. The first negative thought quickly followed, *Oh no, my face is turning red.* A slight tremor appeared in my voice and I thought, *They can see I am nervous and hear it in my voice.* After that, it was a fast spiral down. Pretty soon my face felt like it was on fire. My throat was completely dry, and I had to swallow after what felt like every other word. I was so ashamed that I couldn't look my coworker Rob, who was sitting in the front row, in the eye. As I forced the words out of my mouth, the thoughts were devastating: *I can never face them again after this. I am completely humiliated. My career is over.* Somehow I struggled through the rest of the introduction and handed over the presentation. Sitting slumped in my chair I wished I could disappear into the floor below. It was by far my worst speaking experience ever.

Following the session I met my colleague outside of the conference room. "Rob," I said, "I am so embarrassed about that presentation. I really feel terrible for letting everyone down."

"What are you talking about?" Rob asked. "I thought you were great."

"You must be kidding. I was so embarrassed by how nervous I was; surely it was a disaster."

"No way, Julianne. You came across as very confident, and I could see the group responding positively. We had a great response from everyone, and they are willing to come back for a third session."

"Really?" I was absolutely amazed. Arguably, Rob was overlooking some of the nerves that the audience must have seen during my presentation. However, I will never forget how astonishing it was to learn that he had not seen the absolute magnitude of disaster that I experienced on the inside while delivering that speech.

Instead of feeling devastated, in that moment I chose to congratulate myself for surviving my worst speaking experience ever and to come back to the next working group with my head held high. This strategy proved to work. The third session went smoothly. I was proud of the relationship I developed with the group and of the results achieved. I realized that even if they had seen some of my anxiety maybe it led them to respect me more for persevering and coming back even more prepared and determined to succeed the next time. The speaking disaster I experienced made me realize that I was strong enough to survive a speaking failure and to know it was only me who realized the magnitude of what I was feeling.

The second step in "Daring to Disturb the Universe," after putting the speech into perspective, is to push the comfort zone. This can be done through intentionally reaching for engagements that challenge a speaker's energy and matching it with the emotion and tone of the message to be delivered.

I found a very effective way do this after signing up for an introductory course in acting that pushed my comfort zone when it came to expressing body language. Additionally, I learned valuable techniques for warming up the body to deliver a speech. These exercises, described in detail in the exercise at the end of the chapter, are useful for loosening up and practicing congruently connecting body language and vocal variety with a message.

It felt strange the first time I performed the warm-up exercises in the acting class. *You want me to do what?* was all I could think when the instructor demonstrated what we were to do. However, after giving in and starting to let loose with the rest of the hesitant participants, I began to feel my body let go of the constraints holding me back. At the time I didn't connect these exercises as beneficial to public speaking. However, they felt natural when I warmed up for my next speech. I was amazed at how free I felt on stage. It led to experimenting with use of space. It made me realize the importance of pushing the comfort zone.

These techniques can be learned and practiced without having to take an acting class. The main principle is to experience the sensation of losing the natural inhibitions to body movement and vocal variety felt on stage. The second important benefit is to demonstrate the concept of congruence through exaggerated examples. Follow the instructions in the exercise below and concentrate on congruence between body language and vocal variety. For example, practice making large controlled body movements, experimenting with large vocal sounds to match. Do the same thing with small movements and sounds.

Next, experiment with specific emotions using a full range of body movement and vocal sounds. These exercises are effective as a warm-up to delivering speeches. Many times I sneak off to the bathroom prior to delivering a presentation to do them in private.

With practice all the techniques become easier and more natural.

Dare to Disturb the Universe Exercise:

In this exercise begin to practice pushing the comfort zone. Use the techniques below to calm nerves and focus energy. Think of them as the pre-game warm-up to a successful speech.

1. Mental Preparation:

   - Visualize the "Universe Timeline" discussed at the beginning of the chapter. With the image in mind, pinpoint the speck in time when the speech is to take place. Recognize both how small it actually is and how big your efforts need to be to make an impact.

2. Physical Preparation:

a. Body Language Exercises: Experiment with range of movement. *Note: Make sure to warm up before doing exercises and consult a doctor if unsure you are fit to try them.*

   - Start by walking around in the largest room available. Make sure there is a large, open area.

- Begin moving your arms first in small circles and then in the biggest circles possible while still walking. Remember to change direction occasionally to avoid becoming dizzy.

- Begin to bring your knees up with every step, stretching out the legs.

- Use the full range of motion. Fling your arms, jump around and make the biggest movements possible. *Note: Only move as much as is comfortable for your body.*

- Bring movements down slowly into very small, controlled, and direct movements. Slow down to a stop in one spot.

- Practice going from very small movements to very big movements and back again.

b. Vocal Exercises: Experiment with vocal variety.

- Start by opening the mouth and making any sound that comes to mind.

- Next, think of the alphabet and without fully closing your lips together, make out each sound.

- Go through the same again this time starting as quiet as possible and ending up as loud as possible.

- Finally, play around with different sounds and volumes, going from soft to hard and quiet to loud. Remember that vocal variety includes:

  o Tone: Experiment with variety from soft to harsh sounds.

- o Volume: Experiment with the full range from silence to shouting.
- o Pitch: Experiment with the sound in terms of high and low frequency.

c. Bring it all together: Congruently combine body language with vocal variety.

- • Experiment with exaggerated body language and full vocal variety:

  - o Express anger
  - o Express jubilation
  - o Express fear
  - o Express exhilaration

- • Try a progression and change of emotion:

  - o Express anger turning to joy
  - o Express fear turning to exhilaration

d. Put it to use:

- • When preparing or practicing a speech, experiment bringing in body language and vocal variety. Think about the message and emotion you are trying to convey and focus on congruence in actions and sounds.

The next concept explored is one of the most important speaking tools a speaker has at their disposal. This is a critical component that will enable you to formulate your thoughts in the most effective and engaging manner. Through utilizing this technique, you will learn to…

CHAPTER 3

"Structure Any Speech"

It is best to do things systematically, since we are only human, and disorder is our worst enemy.

– Hesiod (~800 BC)

The two initial principles "Speaking in the Moment" and "Dare to Disturb the Universe" are designed to help a person start speaking without having to think too much about the content of a speech. This method is useful when speakers first begin the practice of flipping the fear. It allows them to speak confidently from the start, since they can more easily relate something from their own experience. It allows them to start pushing the boundaries of their comfort zone.

After experimenting in front of audiences with the first two principles, it's time to make the transition to a more formal speaking environment, such as delivering a technical presentation. Use the first two principles to transition to a more formal setting. Also, the concept of congruence through varying body language, vocal variety, and word choice will be key to making a strong point. This is why it is important to progress through the principles in order.

The third principle, "Structure Your Speech," is based on the concept that a framework can help to organize thoughts and allow a speaker to deliver a clear, concise, and effective speech. The purpose is to ensure that the key message(s) comes across and that the speech makes a point. It is a helpful principle not only for developing a formal presentation, but it can also be used when a person is put on the spot at a meeting. It is useful for calming the nerves when a speaker walks into a large meeting and might be called on to present but is not sure when or how this might happen. I have personally used it over and over again to successfully develop Toastmasters presentations, "Speaking in the Moment" presentations, as well as formal work presentations used to highlight data or deliver specific information.

I first began thinking about the importance of speech structure after listening to a friend in the publishing business. He told me about an experience tuning into a publishing podcast being delivered by a highly qualified and respected individual in the publishing field. When the podcast began, my friend noticed that the presenter, although knowledgeable in his content area, seemed to have no structure at all to his presentation. The result was a much jumbled presentation of some important points hidden within a lot of other, less relevant information. My friend concluded that if the presenter had simply organized his information in a logical sequence, listeners would have been able to pick out the very valuable information that he was trying to share. As it was, he felt the listeners would have been lucky to pick out one or two things from the confusing sequence of delivery.

There is a very simple technique that can help avoid any confusion or disorganization in the delivery of any presentation. It organizes information into five parts:

1. Introduction

2. First Point

3. Second Point

4. Third Point

5. Conclusion

Once speakers have selected a topic, or experience, using the "Speaking in the Moment" technique, they need to select three main focus points to address.

As an example, if speaking about the experience of winning the lottery (as in the first exercise), a speaker might choose to present on three main points:

1) Buying the ticket
2) The moment he or she won the lottery
3) The quandary now faced as everyone they know wants money

Or, if a speaker was putting together a presentation on the status of their department's performance they might want to address:

1) Past department performance

2) The evaluation method used

3) The most recent evaluation results

The key is to pick three main points within the topic that will leave the audience with the key pieces of information the speaker intends to provide. Key points are determined by the individual presenter's preference for the best presentation. They might be ordered chronologically or from the point of greatest impact. Or, the presentation could begin with smaller details and build to the most important point. As long as presentations contain three solid key points, speakers are on the right track.

Once the main key points are organized, a strong introduction is needed. This will be crucial to the presentation as it is the "hook" used to get the audience interested in what the speaker is about to say. For example, my favorite opening statement from a "Speaking in the Moment" speech I have delivered a number of times and have also used in the opening of this book is "I am terrified." I deliver this line and then pause, look at the audience, and repeat: "I am terrified and my heart is racing. My hands are cold and the terror is rising in my throat as I try to speak…"

With this example right of the bat, the intention is to get the audience thinking, "Wow, what is she terrified of?" This serves the purpose of a) getting the audience interested in what comes next and b) setting up the three main content points as the reasons for the terror.

For the conclusion of a speech, "tell the audience what you have told them" by summarizing key information presented in the three points. Do it as concisely as possible and in a way that leaves the audience thinking about the your main message or objective.

One way to practice the principle of structuring a speech is by using the following template:

Introduction…

First…

Second…

Third…

In conclusion…

An easy way to get started is to continue with the sample question from Chapter 1: "What I would do if I won the lottery?" Or, pick another topic that inspires you. Start by choosing three main points and then sketching out the responses, including an introduction and conclusion in the template provided. Of importance is that only one or two key words need be used to summarize the content of each main point. This is useful because key words can be used later to populate a visual presentation, such as PowerPoint or speaking notes. Concise key words can also serve as visual reminders for speakers, if needed, so that they do not have to fumble around with long written notes. For example, concise key words that illustrate the example above might include the following:

Introduction: I am elated

First: Quit job

Second: New home

Third: Beach every day

Conclusion: Elated, quit job, new home, beach every day.

With this structure, the speaker can look at the key words and speak to the points without having to read from notes as long as they have prepared and have an idea of the content that fits the points.

This technique can be used when preparing for a formal speech and also, as mentioned earlier, when preparing for a meeting where the speaker may or may not be required to participate. For many, it provokes anxiety to sit around a meeting table and know that at any minute they might be asked to provide input or present informally on a topic. The anxiety is increased because no one knows when or how this will happen. But it can be helpful to fill out a response template based on what the speaker thinks they might be asked during the meeting. This helps both to organize the speaker's thoughts before going in and to increase confidence as the speaker is now prepared in case they are put on the spot.

While attending my second corporate meeting after receiving a job in business development, I recognized the value of this technique. A week prior, while attending a similar meeting, my palms were sweating and my hands were shaking with the thought of being called on and asked to present. All I could think about was the look on my colleagues' faces when they saw how red my face would be. *Please, please don't ask me.* I silently wished that I would not be put on the spot to give an update on my department in front of all of these people. The boardroom seemed so small, so hot. I felt trapped. I was certain that no words would come out of my mouth if I tried to speak. Thankfully, I was not asked to speak at the meeting that day, and as I contemplated the source of my anxiety after the meeting, I concluded that it was a case of not being prepared for what I would have said if asked to present. The next week, when the second meeting came up I made sure I was ready. Prior to the meeting, I prepared a template structure of three key points. Each point served to illustrate how my department was functioning. There was one positive point, one point that illustrated an issue, and a third point detailing how we planned to proceed. When I sat in the second meeting, I could again feel the anxiety building in my body as updates were requested around the table. This time I was called on, and although I felt nervous and am sure my face did turn red, I managed to deliver a well-thought-out and structured update that was met with approval from my boss. Using the structure had provided me with a roadmap for my thoughts and allowed for clear focus points. This is a technique I now use every time I am asked to attend a meeting where I might be asked to present.

Once familiar with the format it becomes a logical way to organize a speech even when it's impromptu, or unexpected. For example, a speaker is attending a meeting and his or her boss asks the person to provide some thoughts on something they had not prepared for. When familiar with the template the speaker can quickly think about the question just asked and choose three highlights. The speaker can then introduce the points in the form of an introduction followed by a brief discussion on each point with a summary conclusion. The result will sound like the speaker has really put some thought into the response rather than starting to ramble about the first thing that comes to mind. This technique will not only impress an audience into thinking the speaker really has an organized way of presenting, but it will also allow the audience members to more easily interpret the information and allow them to quickly highlight three main points to take away.

The better speakers become at structuring speeches, the more natural it becomes, and they won't need to always include the structure words in a presentation.

Structure Your Speech Exercise:

1. Continue the example from Chapter 1, "What I would do if I won the lottery?" Or, summarize a new topic below:

_____

_____

2. Structure the speech in the outline provided below. For each topic key word, bring in at least one description sentence (I see, I hear, I feel, I

smell, I taste, I think) from the first chapter. Use these descriptors to build around the key words and develop the speech.

Speech Structure Outline:

Introduction: Key word (e.g., elated) used in an attention-grabbing introductory sentence (e.g., "I am elated") and what you are going to tell the audience in an introduction of the three main topic points, e.g., "I am now going to tell you why I am elated in three key points."

_____

_____

- First: (e.g., Quit job)

    _____

I see: _____ I hear: _____

I feel: _____ I smell: _____

I taste: _____ I think: _____

- Second: (e.g., New house)

    _____

I see: _____ I hear: _____

I feel: _____ I smell: _____

I taste: _____ I think: _____

- Third: (e.g., Beach every day)

_____

I see: _____ I hear: _____

I feel: _____ I smell: _____

I taste: _____ I think: _____

Conclusion: Key summary word re-cap and why this is important to the speaker, e.g., "I am elated because I quit my job, bought a new house, and go to the beach every day. This means freedom and the life I have always dreamed of."

_____

_____

_____

Once you have mastered the art of speech structure, there is another critical element that can help ensure success before you even reach the podium. This principal is applied when you begin to…

CHAPTER 4

"Dress for Success"

Clothes make the man. Naked people have little or no influence on society.

– Mark Twain (1835 – 1910)

The fourth principle, "Dress for Success," builds on the philosophy of "Fake it until you make it." It is important to begin achieving success and confidence before stepping on the stage even though a speaker has gained the tools to put a speech together and developed the courage to deliver it.

Imagine walking into a room with shoulders slumped, face looking down to the ground, and holding a crumpled piece of paper with both hands. You're wearing an old, wrinkled shirt and your oldest running shoes, your trousers are stained in the front, and you forgot to comb your hair that morning.

Dressing that way would create lack of confidence and low energy to begin with, followed by thoughts such as "I hope no one notices me walking into this room." Or worse, what if you actually ended up having to give a speech?

Imagine walking into the same room standing up straight and tall, head looking straight in front and eyes ready to meet the glance of anyone who is watching. You have a warm smile at the ready, and there is an energy behind it that says "I am happy and excited to be here." You are wearing a newly pressed suit that fits well and a crisp white shirt that felt good the minute you put it on. Your shoes are polished and your feet move quickly and confidently entering the room. Your hands are empty and are resting confidently at your side, carrying no notes. You are an expert in the material you are about to present.

Imagine audience members in each of the two scenes described above. In the first one when the audience members see the speaker walk into a room to deliver a presentation looking at the floor, avoiding eye contact, and being sloppy in appearance, they might wonder if staying in their seats would be beneficial. In the second scene, however, audience members might sit up a bit to meet the eyes of the speaker who walks in with a smile bright with energy. More of the audience might stick around to hear the speaker.

The point is speakers set themselves up for success or failure in speaking, as in most things, before even beginning to speak. It starts with speech preparation providing them with knowledge to share. But even earlier, perhaps the previous night before climbing into bed, they give a confident smile to the mirror that says "I can do this." Maybe just before confident speakers drift off to sleep they envision the feeling of success they will enjoy after delivering a well-received speech. All of the previous preparations, including body language and dress, in addition to the speech itself create the energy a speaker brings into a room.

At eighteen I learned the lesson of perception. I had walked into my first Dale Carnegie public speaking course. I was terrified of public speaking at that time and had asked my parents if they would pay for the course so that I could gain confidence for the presentations I knew I would have to give in my first year of university. I've never forgotten what I learned in that first session. Sitting at the back of the room I was nervous and unsure of the experience that was awaiting me. When a businessman, dressed in a very sharp looking suit, tie, and polished shoes, came into the room I automatically assumed he was the instructor. To my surprise, he walked into the room, focused on the empty chair beside me, and sat down. "Hi, my name is Roy." I was almost too surprised to respond and felt my cheeks flushing. "Hi Roy, my name is Julianne."

Over that first session, I learned a very important lesson in perception. When Roy walked into the room he stood tall, and his presence spoke of confidence. His clothes were professional and thoughtfully put together, his shoes were polished, and he looked like he was ready to step up and command a boardroom meeting. It was with great shock and amazement that as the session began and we went through the exercises of introducing ourselves and began to practice public speaking techniques that I learned that Roy was more terrified than I was of getting up in front of that group of people to speak. Over the next three months of the course, Roy and I became friends, and I learned that his fear of public speaking made him sure he would faint or that simply no words would come out when he tried to speak. He had a respectable job in business in the city, but he avoided speaking in public at all costs, even to the point of negatively impacting his career. He had finally decided to try to face his fear so that he would be able to stand up and speak at his daughter's upcoming wedding.

I can still picture Roy and have never forgotten the lesson he taught me. Not only should I not assume that everyone around me who looks professional is a more confident speaker than me, but also I learned that in order to increase my audience's perception of my confidence level, I must walk into a room as Roy did: dressed professionally, looking straight ahead, and demonstrating an air of confidence, even if I am completely terrified of what I am about to do.

At first when people challenge their fear of public speaking, they can take the lesson from Roy and use it to their advantage. Before an important meeting that might require them to speak or before delivering a presentation they are nervous about they can help the process by a confident image. They can put thought into what they will wear the night before the presentation. They can spend time ironing a shirt so that it looks crisp, and they can wear their best suit or jacket or skirt and put it on with confidence knowing the audience will notice. Also, they can get up thirty minutes early and spend time doing their hair and making sure they feel good when walking out the door.

If unsure of where to start this process of becoming confident, select someone who impresses you in your field of work or anyone in the world to emulate. Make a case study of them. How does the person dress for a presentation? How does the person carry themselves when he or she walks into a room? What is it about the person's appearance before speaking that makes people sit up and pay attention thinking, "Wow, this person looks great, and I want to know what he or she is going to say?" Once you have an image of what success looks like, begin taking steps to put yourself in that same place. Maybe this means going out and spending a bit more on a "presentation suit" or getting a new haircut or new computer case. Whatever it is, spend time on appearance so that when walking into a room for that first speech, you're confident of looking professional. Preparing for success means that no matter what the speech is about, you will be starting with the confidence borne of knowing you look great and of knowing no one is able to notice all the nerves inside.

Dress for Success Exercise:

1. Visualize: Picture a person who represents success in the area you

   wish to be successful in and write his or her name here.

   _____

2. Describe: With the picture of this person in mind, describe at least five things about the person that you notice or admire (e.g., clothing, posture, hairstyle, facial expression, voice, etc.).

- _____

- _____

- _____

- _____

- _____

3. Plan and Act: Describe how, when, and where you are going to adopt or emulate the above five points in a way that you are comfortable with and that reflects the vision of success you had in mind when picturing the individual. Remember, the more specific, the more likely you are to follow through.

- _____

- _____

- _____

- _____

The first four principals will set you on the path to success. However, in order to unlock your fullest potential, you must learn to…

CHAPTER 5

"Set Your Compass to Success"

"The life given us, by nature is short; but the memory of a well-spent life
is eternal."

– Marcus Tullius Cicero

At this point, those armed with a toolkit for successful speaking, including having practiced, have likely caught a glimpse of what "flipping the fear" feels like. It might be elusive at first, but it is important to notice and to celebrate small moments when enjoyment overcomes nervousness. Even if fleeting at first, these moments will grow with continued practice to the point that it feels like, "Hey, I can do this!" With increasing challenge, those who stick with the process will be amazed at how far they get both in speaking and in other areas of life.

This last principle is key to ensuring continual movement forward as a successful public speaker and also toward larger goals in a professional and personal life. It involves practicing everything learned so far and combining skills to bring alive a vision of success for the future. The purpose of "Setting Your Compass to Success" is not only to practice all of the principles learned so far but to also create a tangible goal to move toward. The premise that "thoughts become things" will help to drive careers or personal goals to reality.

I think back to the most magical day of my life...

I can't believe I am here! Looking around I see limestone buildings with funny pointed tops and crests and imposing black and steel doors closing off the wonders beyond to the cobblestone streets. A cherry tree on the street corner is in full bloom with pink blossoms in vivid contrast to the historical structures surrounding it. All around I hear students on the street, talking as they walk past or cycle by, their books either on their backs or in the baskets on their bikes. I feel the August sun on my face, and as I inhale I think that the air is sweeter here and more alive. It is as if learning is tangible in the air and all I can think, all I can feel, is that I want to be a part of it. Tilting my head back I look up to the sky. The cloud formations are clear and honest in how they look back at me from the pale, yet sharp blue sky, and they seem to hear my prayer: *Please, I would do anything if in my lifetime I am given the opportunity to study here.* It is as if a whisper comes alive from the thought and travels up to the clouds, although never escaping from my lips. Tangible, the feeling of wanting that dream is in my body. I can see myself on these same streets, but as a student, as someone with a right and a pass to what lies beyond those secret and imposing doors.

Without question, the most valuable tool I have learned, and one that can be used by anyone to move forward toward achieving goals, is the power of visualization. I learned the value of this principle after visualizing myself as a student at Oxford University. At the time, this seemed an unrealistic and distant dream. Living and working as a nurse in Canada, studying at Oxford seemed completely unattainable. However, after I stood in the street and visualized what this dream would feel like coming true, a strange thing happened. Little by little my circumstances changed. As time passed, I found myself in a position to apply for a master's degree. Then, an amazing mentor suggested I aim at the school I wanted the most. Finally, after a full year of studying for the entrance exam, writing my application, and visualizing the moment it would happen, I was accepted.

The process of visualizing a goal and "Setting Your Compass to Success" follows a simple method. First of all, put yourself "in the moment." This time, however, describe a future experience rather than a past or present experience. Visualize the moment you achieve success in the experience and describe it. Just as in "Speaking in the Moment," bring the experience to life through the five senses: What do you see, hear, feel, touch, taste and think? The power in this exercise comes from the emotion and feeling put into description. Bring the moment when the dream comes to life into reality through your words. Use as much description as possible in as many pages as it takes.

When you have a goal pictured vividly in your mind, the next step is to "Dare to Disturb the Universe." If imagining getting a degree, pick the school of your dreams. If imagining learning to swim, picture swimming across the English Channel. If imagining learning to paint, see the painting hanging in the Louvre museum in Paris. Goals, and therefore success and accomplishments, are only held back by the limits of the imagination. Now is the time to disturb the universe by challenging the mind to come up with an amazing future. Get creative as you imagine doing what you have always wanted.

Once described in detail and taking form on the page, the goal can come to life. The next step is to structure the visual description in a speech. This will not only give the goal further tangible form, but sharing the speech with an audience will help to hold the goal-setter accountable going forward.

To structure the speech start by asking what are three main points to illustrate about achieving the goal? Perhaps this includes the following:

1) The moment when deciding to focus on the goal,
2) Describing a challenge faced in attempting to achieve the goal
3) Describing the moment when the goal is finally achieved

Or, it might focus on three key points in the moment the goal becomes reality. For example, in the moment describe the following:

1) Who is with you and what this means to you
2) How you feel at the time and how this contrasts with how you felt before
3) What accomplishing this dream means for you going forward

After structuring the goal in a speech, arguably the most important speech you could give, the next step is to go out and find an audience. Whether it is to family, friends, coworkers, or to a Toastmasters group, the challenge is to practice this speech, dress up for success, and walk into a room to deliver it as the vision for your success going forward. You might be surprised by the support received from an audience who feels the passion and enthusiasm put into the vision described. Once out in the open, this vision will be well on the way to becoming reality.

Set Your Compass to Success Exercise:

1. Vision Plan: Use the entire space provided (and more if you want) to describe in detail using the "Speaking in the Moment" principle, exactly what you feel, hear, see, taste, smell, and think in your vision of success.

_____

_____

_____

_____

_____

_____

_____

_____

_____

_____

2. Speech Structure Outline:

Introduction: Key word used in an attention-grabbing introductory
sentence followed by what you are going to tell the audience:

_____

_____

- First (key word):

_____

I see: _____

I hear: _____

I feel: _____

I smell: _____

I taste: _____

I think:_____

- Second (key word):

_____

I see: _____

I hear: _____

I feel: _____

I smell: _____

I taste: _____

I think:_____

- Third (key word):

     _____

I see: _____

I hear: _____

I feel: _____

I smell: _____

I taste: _____

I think: _____

Conclusion: Key summary word recap and why this is important to you:

_____

_____

_____

_____

_____

3. Setting SMART Goals to Get There

Now, take the time to congratulate yourself for getting this far. You have come a long way, and putting thoughts into written words is a powerful way to start a path of action. Goal-setting is a very important way to ensure progress. In the exercise below, turn visions into actionable steps that can then become reality.

Setting SMART goals means:

- S – Specific
- M – Measureable
- A – Achievable
- R – Realistic, Relevant
- T – Have a specific Time frame

Example of a SMART goal: By February 2013 I will join Toastmasters, and in my first month with the group (by March 15, 2013) I will complete my first Toastmasters Icebreaker speech.

Below, set at least three goals that will specifically move you toward the set vision. Use this exercise over and over again to move toward the vision and into the future. Ideally, set short-term, mid-term, and long-term goals.

Goal #1:

_____

_____

Goal #2:

_____

_____

Goal #3:

_____

_____

4. Act

Now is the time to act. Take the SMART goals and, with the vision in mind, put them into action and be prepared to celebrate success!

CHAPTER 6

"Practice, Practice, Practice"

Do what you know and perception is converted into character.
– Ralph Waldo Emerson (1803 – 1882)

To this point, five skills and principles for channeling nervous energy and "flipping the fear" of public speaking have been described. Now it is time to get practical. The final element comes into play when a new speaker starts working with the concepts and is beginning to experience "flipping" public speaking fear into genuine enthusiasm. Otherwise described as the "maintenance" phase of the process, it can be related to the stage people enter after starting an exercise routine and begin to see results. At this point they may look in the mirror and think, "Wow, I am looking good." They might also be tempted to think, "I am seeing such good results now that it won't hurt if I skip my workout today." They start to feel overconfident and falsely believe the effort put in initially will be magically sustained. It's easy to guess what happens next.

Here is an example that brought home the importance of this principle:

It was the first class of the adult weight loss program I had been hired to teach. As this was my third time through the ten-session program, I was starting to feel pretty confident. The extreme feeling of nervousness I had in the first program was beginning to translate into energy. I could see results in increased engagement from participants and positive evaluations from the sessions.

This program was different from the first two because it began after Christmas with a three-week break in between. After finishing the second series on a high, I went into the break feeling pretty confident about taking on the teaching role. Over the break I let my mind wander and spent time with family. Somehow that first session after Christmas snuck up on me without much thought.

I brought out my lesson plan notes and thought *Ahh yes, I remember this and how well it went over last time. No need to spend too much time on it this time around.* I reviewed the notes briefly, packed up my things, and headed off to teach the class. When I arrived something was different. My supervisor entered the room as I was preparing for the participants to arrive. "Hi, Julianne. Welcome back from the break. I was just so busy all through the first and second programs that you were teaching that I never had the chance to come down and watch you teach. I was thinking that today would be the perfect opportunity if you don't mind me sitting in."

"Um, sure, of course I don't mind." I was surprised by her visit. It was at this point that things started to change. When I saw her sit down at the back of the classroom and the new participants started to arrive, I started to get nervous. Gone was the confidence I had felt that morning when I barely glanced at my preparation notes, and gone with it were the words I was so sure would come out right when I started to teach the class. The rest of the class played out as you can imagine. I barely made it through and felt embarrassed and ashamed because it was not nearly up to the standards of the first two programs. Also, at multiple points I lost my thoughts—once so badly my supervisor had to step in and add to the lesson.

What I learned, and have since learned over and over again, thankfully fewer times, is that no matter how confident speakers are on a subject they always need to ensure adequate preparation. In the process of flipping the fear of public speaking, the need to constantly practice will never go away. Just as the person who begins exercising regularly cannot one day decide to stop and expect to maintain the same level of fitness, neither can the public speaker stop speaking and expect to maintain the same level of confidence.

It was interesting to read Malcom Gladwell's book *Outliers* and the concept of "10,000 hours" after discovering the necessity of practice. Gladwell theorizes that to be exceptionally good at something requires more hours of practice to make a person exceptional, rather than natural talent. Related to speaking, this means that no matter how terrified of speaking a person is and no matter how little talent they feel they have, the more they practice and get outside of the comfort zone, the better they will become. One day they will even have people looking to them for advice on how to develop the speaking skill demonstrated.

It is true that even the experts need to continually practice and find new ways of challenging themselves. It is easy to reach a level of speaking that feels comfortable and forget to keep looking for new challenges. A speaker will only continue developing if they are challenged to step outside of the comfort zone over and over. The comfort zone will keep expanding the more it is challenged.

Finally, as speakers progress they might have times when the nervousness returns and creates a terrible speaking experience. Speakers might begin to do a presentation they have done one hundred times before and all of a sudden feel that old panic creeping in. This is normal. The upward slope of progression will likely include downward points, but success is found when speakers keep showing up and continuing to challenge the fear of speaking.

Many organizations exist that can help new speakers. Toastmasters and Dale Carnegie are two great speaking organizations for a more structured approach.

But a person can still begin by speaking to the bedroom wall. Whatever provides a safe practice outlet will work. The key is to prepare for a speech and get started speaking out loud. Once started, the challenge will be to seek out speaking experiences and opportunities where you are in control before being asked or forced into delivering a presentation unprepared.

The Scale of Increasing Challenge

Start practicing speaking continuously and challenge the comfort zone by progressing through the scale of increasing challenge below. The challenge level increases with a) audience size b) formality of environment c) technical difficulty of presentation and d) level of consequence riding on the ability to influence through the speech.

a.   Practice an outlined speech in your mind.
b.   In a small room alone, practice an outlined speech out loud.
c.   In a small room, invite a non-intimidating audience, such as a cat or dog, and practice an outlined speech out loud.
d.   At home, invite a human audience of one who you feel comfortable around, such as a spouse or house mate, and practice an outlined speech out loud.
e.   At home, invite two or more humans who you feel comfortable around and practice an outlined speech out loud.
f.   In a new environment, find an audience of two or more, such as a Toastmasters club, and deliver an outlined speech.
g.   In a formal environment, such as at work, deliver a prepared speech
h.   Prepare and deliver a new speech to a medium- to large-size audience (20–100), such as at a wedding or large corporate event.
i.   Prepare and deliver a presentation to a large audience (500+) on any topic, such as a keynote or graduation address.

j.   Prepare and deliver a formal speech under high pressure to a large audience when there is a lot riding on your ability to influence, such as a political speech or memorial on a national scale.

CONCLUSION

> "The future has several names. For the weak, it is impossible; for the
> fainthearted, it is unknown; but for the valiant, it is ideal."
>
> – Victor Hugo

The principles of flipping the fear can be used for more than public speaking. The skills are transferable to any number of personal and professional challenges. Vision planning and setting goals for the future inside an expanding comfort zone have the potential to create far-reaching success.

I had the opportunity to test all five principles of Flip the Fear this past fall when I was asked to deliver a toast to the bride at my cousin's wedding. By this point in my career, I was relatively comfortable with speaking to corporate audiences in a professional setting, but for some reason the prospect of speaking in front of family was more intimidating. Growing up, I was terrified that one day I might be asked to speak at a wedding and finally that day had arrived. Luckily, I had three months to prepare. I procrastinated for the first month, but the speech was always on my mind. At the start of the second month, I decided it was time to get to work. As it was a personal and fairly informal speech, I wanted to incorporate personal experience through speaking in the moment. I also knew that the speech needed a strong structure. On this basis I started with the concept of three main points and thought about what kind of moments needed to be shared. As my cousin is very musically talented, I thought it would be relevant to build the speech around her early musical influence. I chose three periods from our childhood represented by music from the time. Next, I further divided each period into three main points: a description of the music, current wardrobe, and activities from the time. I wrote out my speech structure in key words and brainstormed description around each point based on "Speaking in the Moment." Once the structure was in place, I started my practice regime. Each day, I recited the speech in my mind in entirety at least once. This was a lot of practice, but I was anxious about the speech, so it felt relevant. With each recital my confidence grew.

As the day approached, I put thought into my wardrobe and how I would physically present the speech at the wedding. The wedding had a Halloween theme, so it was easy to put some fun into this part. I even recruited my brother to perform part of the song "The Time Warp" at the end of the speech as a special tribute to the bride. This helped to alleviate my anxiety as it brought an element of fun. Two weeks prior to the wedding, I started to practice the speech out loud with an audience. I recruited family and friends and also practiced alone when no one was available. The week prior to the speech I knew it so well that I was able to embellish the details while performing rather than concentrating on remembering the descriptions. It began to be fun.

Music was the key addition to support the speech, so I ensured that the songs were in order on an iPod. I also checked the wedding venue to ensure that this technology would work and that a way existed to play the music. I also recruited my brother to key the music while we practiced just as it would be presented at the wedding.

I made sure to pack my full outfit and iPod for travel to the wedding. I also scheduled one final practice round with my brother at the setting. We would not be able to see the room until just before the wedding, so we made sure to discuss how we would set up with different scenarios in mind.

Finally, the day arrived. I was nervous but excited, and I had a sense of security knowing that I had invested all I could in preparation and practice. The toast was scheduled for after the wedding ceremony during the meal. I found it hard to eat, but made sure I did. Likewise, I made sure I had enough water to drink before the speech and also asked for a five-minute warning before speaking so that I could stop eating and ensure my throat was clear.

Then, it was time. "Now, Julianne will deliver the toast to the bride." I took my water and key word notes but could feel the heat rising in my face as I walked up to the podium. After a deep breath, I began: "I am so nervous." Pause. "But so excited!" From that moment, my voice was strong and I was in the moment delivering the key point descriptions to the audience. An occasional thought of my red face crept in, but I pushed it away and concentrated on connecting with the audience. By the time the speech was over and the "Time Warp" began, I was thoroughly enjoying myself. When the bride and bridesmaid joined my brother and me during the dance and I saw the smiles and laughter from the audience, I knew the performance had been a success.

Collapsing into my chair after the performance, I took a deep breath. Relaxation and a sense of accomplishment washed over my body. *I did it.* Similar to the day I ran the grade-six foot race, I liked the feeling.

As a new speaker, be kind to yourself as flipping the fear is not easy. Remember also that speakers with a lot of nervous energy have the most potential to become great. Sustained effort and perseverance combined with an image of success will flip negative energy into positive enthusiasm and the power to persuade an audience. If after using some of these methods it still seems impossible to get up in front of an audience to speak, it means an even more fulfilling journey ahead for those who continue to commit to try. Start with small, achievable steps. Speak to the wall, a cat, or audience of one, and build from there. Celebrate success no matter how small and don't worry about temporary setbacks. They will dissipate by continually seeking out other challenges. Always concentrate on moving forward.

EPILOGUE

Working on the final version of this book, I encountered a new speaking challenge. After battling cancer, my great aunt passed away, and I was asked to read a eulogy sent by my uncle from Bangladesh. Having just completed work on "The Scale of Increasing Challenge," I was acutely aware that this was the highest level of challenge I had ever faced. The thought of speaking at the funeral was challenging because of the emotions involved. I wanted to make my great aunt and family proud and to be strong. It was also challenging because I had been out of speaking practice for three weeks during Christmas and had not spoken publically for two months. Driving to Edmonton with my mom, I felt the adrenaline hit my bloodstream the moment she said, "You know, your uncle asked if you would read the eulogy." My initial reaction was, "Why doesn't the priest read it?" However, the more I thought about it, I knew it was a responsibility to my aunt and family as well as a challenge. But from that moment on until I stood up to the podium, I was full of nervous energy.

Over the three days before the funeral, I took my own advice to heart. Using the "Emergency Speech Preparation" formula, I made a plan and then scheduled three practice readings with an audience of family. I planned to be dressed for success in appropriate attire, and I ensured that I had a bottle of water and a copy of the eulogy to take to the funeral. Most of all, I made peace with self-doubt and put faith in the idea that I had been asked to read the eulogy because I could handle it and that with the right intentions in my heart, it would go well.

The night before the funeral I pictured myself standing at the podium projecting a message of strength and comfort through my uncle's words. I visualized my family in the audience, the surroundings, and the words on the eulogy page. I imagined the feeling of strength I would have reading the words. Falling asleep, I promised to do my best and trusted that I had the strength.

The morning of the funeral my heart was pumping and hands were sweating. I dressed and ate a proper breakfast even though it was hard to swallow. I took time to make myself presentable and kept in mind the image of strength and comfort I wanted to project and rejected any self-doubts creeping in.

Feeling strong walking up to the front and beginning to speak, I made a point to project my voice to the back of the room. Afterward, I was filled with sadness as well as pride for having delivered the tribute as I had envisioned.

The nervousness I had felt preparing to read the eulogy was as great as before any other speech in my life. However, by following the principles of Flip the Fear, I challenged myself and successfully accomplished the task. It was further testament to both the continual challenge of speaking and the effectiveness of the Flip the Fear principles.

Appendix A:

Emergency Successful Speech Plan

This Emergency Successful Speech Plan is designed for those times when a speaker is "caught" and asked to give a speech with little time to prepare. This speech plan will help a speaker to "set up for success" when the pressure is on. With less than three weeks before a speech, try to get at least three practice sessions in and complete as many additional bullet points as possible.

Three to four weeks before the speech:

- Become familiar with the speech topic if it is provided; otherwise, start brainstorming potential topics.

    o For an informal speech, use concepts of "Speaking in the Moment" and try to think of experiences to use that would be appropriate to share.

- Once the topic is in place, use the "Structure Your Speech" outline to structure the speech into an audience-grabbing introduction, three main points, and conclusion.

- If visual aids will be used, put the speech into an initial draft PowerPoint presentation based on the structure provided.

- Begin to practice the speech. Run through the speech in your mind. Initially, this is easiest when engaged in a physical activity, such as walking, running, gardening, etc. This will help take initial anxiety away from practicing.

Two to three weeks before the speech:

- Start to practice the speech out loud using summary notes of the three key points or using a visual presentation. Start by practicing alone in a room and then recruiting a small audience you are comfortable with: cat, dog, spouse, housemates, friends, etc.

- Plan to use the key points of "Dressing for Success." If a haircut or new outfit is needed, get it.

- Ensure any PowerPoint presentations are finalized.

One week before the speech:

- Set aside at least three blocks of time to run through your speech in its entirety. Don't skip parts; be disciplined to try to deliver it every time as if you are on stage. For as many of these times as possible, try to use an audience.

- If the venue for the speech is nearby, check out the room beforehand to become familiar with the layout.

One day before the speech:

- For a PowerPoint presentation, ensure that it is on a USB stick and also have a backup plan, such as emailing the presentation to yourself and the host.

Evening before the speech:

- Run through the presentation as if it is the actual time to deliver it. Have as many people in the "audience" as possible. Explain to them that this is the last time and ply them with chocolate if required.

- Ensure clothing is prepared for the presentation. This includes ironing a shirt and shining shoes, if needed. Try on the clothes, especially if they are new or haven't been worn for a while, to avoid any last-minute wardrobe emergencies.

- Lying in bed, visualize travelling to deliver the speech, preparing at the location, and finally walking out on stage and delivering the best presentation possible. Be as imaginative as possible, visualizing the smiles on the audience members' faces and the amazing feeling of success when the speech is over and you did a fantastic job.

Day of the speech:

- Get up early. Provide extra time so there is no rush during last-minute stops or unplanned wardrobe changes.

- Eat. Even if you can't stomach the thought of food because of nerves, make sure to eat something that will provide needed energy and enthusiasm to share.

- Exercise. If possible, get out and do some physical activity to get the nerves under control and regulate body temperature. Plan enough time to shower and prepare after the activity.

- Dress for success. Take time getting ready and enjoy the feeling of the prepared clothes. Look in the mirror before leaving and be pleased with what you see. You are already successful at this point.

- Bring water. Likely there will be water at the event, but it is always helpful to know there is some available.

- Set a positive frame of mind during travel to the event. Listen to an energetic song or relaxing music. Do whatever is required to get into the right mood.

- At the venue, make sure the environment is prepared. This includes setting up the visual presentation if necessary, storing personal belongings, and visiting the washroom. Importantly, if someone is hosting you, make sure to introduce yourself and provide any last-minute details to the host.

Waiting to speak:

- Follow the speech relaxation exercises (see Appendix B) when sitting and waiting to present to calm last-minute nerves.

- Speak successfully because, when prepared, a speaker has succeeded before even standing up.

Appendix B:

Speaking Relaxation Exercises

You are sitting on stage in front of an audience as the last presenter scheduled. Everyone who has spoken so far seemed amazingly confident and put together. You feel nerves starting to build. Breathing is speeding up, palms are getting sweaty, and hands are getting cold. You start to think, "Can I really do this?"

To help you calm these last-minute nerves, try the following relaxation exercises. They can be done right from the chair you sit in while waiting to present.

1. Breathing for relaxation:

    a. Take note of breathing and consciously try to slow it down.

b. When breathing in, draw the breath to the bottom of the diaphragm and fill the lungs.

c. Hold breath for a pause at the end of inhalation.

d. On exhalation slightly purse the lips and breathe out slowly. As you are breathing out, make sure to exhale slightly longer than you inhaled while imagining all of the nervous energy sailing out of the body on the air being released.

e. Continue to take steady, deep breaths and exhale just slightly longer than you inhale. With every breath, feel yourself becoming more relaxed.

2. Use muscles to release nervous energy:

a. Sitting in a chair, pay attention to the muscles in the body. Make a conscious effort to relax them. Let the shoulders naturally sink into position, put the feet flat on the floor, and relax the hands/arms into the lap.

b. Starting with the toes and feet, clench the muscles as hard as possible, hold for a pause, and then relax. When relaxing the muscles, feel the nervous energy leaving the body. Remember to breathe while performing the exercises. Breathe in when clenching and exhale out as you relax.

c. Work your way up from the toes and feet: ankles and calves, upper legs (both front quadriceps and back hamstrings), bottom (gluteus maximus), core abdominals and lower back, upper back and chest, shoulders and upper arms, lower arms and hands, and neck and face.

d. With each muscle group, clench, hold, and relax. Feel the body becoming more and more relaxed as the nervous energy leaves when the muscles release.

e. When reaching the top of the body (neck and face) follow clenching and relaxing with long inhalations and slightly longer exhalations as described above.

f. Repeat as required to achieve a relaxed state, so that you are ready to step up when the time comes.

Appendix C:

Tricks of the Trade to Calm the Nerves

These tricks of the trade are tested and true to help alleviate anxiety for those just beginning to speak and/or who are extremely anxious. They are for those days when, despite all the preparation, nervousness sets in.

For fear of red face:

- Apply makeup concealer in a greenish hue. It is available at any makeup counter and used as a combatant against red skin.

- For long hair, style and wear down. Be careful it is not in face or distracting.

- Wear something interesting, but not distracting, to take the attention away from the face. Stay away from red and pink colors to draw attention.

- Request the lights be slightly dimmed. Do this only if appropriate for the venue and presentation, such as when delivering a visual presentation that the audience can see better with dim lights.

Fear of dry/sticky throat:

- Drink lots of water and remain hydrated. Keep water near while presenting and take sips as required.

- Don't eat anything sticky or dry, such as bananas or baked goods, less than thirty minutes before presenting.

- Gargle. If it feels something is stuck in your throat, gargle with water.

Fear of shaking voice:

- Speak loudly. Focus on speaking to the back of the room without actually shouting. Speaking loudly will keep the voice strong and will also help those at the back to hear.

- Ensure water is on hand and take a drink if you need to pause and regain composure.

Fear of forgetting your place or not being able to carry on:

- First, realize that with adequate preparation, this is very likely not going to happen. However, just in case:

    o   Have a list of questions for the audience on hand. If you do lose your place or need a moment to catch your breath, ask the audience a question, or ask them to consider something for a moment and to volunteer a comment or question.

    o   Turn the tables. Ask the audience to turn to a neighbor and discuss something in the speech. Ask them to prepare a response back to the group. Make this appropriate for any point during the presentation so that it can be used when needed.

    o   Have on hand a video clip, or other relevant media clip, that you could play at any time.

Fear of sweating:

- Wear dark clothing to avoid showing signs of sweating. Ensure that you can take a jacket/sweater off without fear of showing stains when too hot.

- Keep a handkerchief in a pocket in case you need to subtly dab the forehead for sweat. Try to do this while the audience has attention on something else, such as after asking them to look at visual slides or after asking them to discuss something in groups.

General fear:

- Introduce as many appropriate visuals in the presentation as possible so that the spotlight will be on them and the attention on whatever you are showing.

- Bring in as much experience/passion as possible. The more genuinely excited you are, the easier it will be to "flip the fear" and forget about nerves.

- Get the audience laughing. If possible, insert a funny slide or joke at some point during the presentation. This will help lighten both your mood and that of the audience.

- Follow the Successful Speech Plan to be confident in your preparation.

Overall, make sure you look great. This way you will feel great, which is one of the best ways to set yourself up for success.

About the Author

Harnessing the power of fear, Julianne Kissack overcame an intense terror of public speaking to fuel and achieve dreams she once could only imagine. Starting her career as a Registered Nurse in Calgary, Canada, she travelled to the United Kingdom in 2008 to pursue an MBA at Oxford University. Both during her time nursing and as a Healthcare Consultant, working for companies such as the British Medical Association, the UK National Health Service, BMI Healthcare, Fraser Health, and Allscripts, she has used public speaking as a tool to empower patients and also to achieve success in the corporate world. Through her five principles of "Fliping the Fear" and a large dose of energy and enthusiasm, the author captivates, motivates, and inspires audiences to see fear as an opportunity for growth and to live their best life.

CPSIA information can be obtained
at www.ICGtesting.com
Printed in the USA
FFOW02n0213090817
38655FF